Get It ~~Write~~ Right!

Spelling

Mechanics

Usage

Proofreading

For students, parents, & teachers:
Exercises to teach writing skills in the early grades
Preparation for standardized testing

Mary S. Schatz

A Breath of Fresh Air
Garlic Press

D1227802

Thanks to all the teachers who advised me and tested this workbook especially Gwen Danielson, Susan Scott, Judy Shoemaker, Suzanne Spencer, and Robyn Wallace. Special thanks to Jane Perkins who is all-knowing in matters of grammar and writing.

Published by
Garlic Press
605 Powers St.
Eugene, OR 97401

ISBN 1-930820-48-8
Order Number GP-148
Printed in China

To the Teacher

This set of exercises is designed to teach many of the writing skills commonly addressed in the standardized testing of the early grades.

The first section of each unit is **Spelling.** Students learn to recognize the correct spelling of frequently used words. Basic patterns such as short-vowel, long-vowel, and blends as well as rules appropriate for the early grades are stressed.

The second section of each unit concentrates on **Mechanics.** Students learn to punctuate and capitalize correctly. The notion of a complete sentence is introduced, and alphabetization is taught.

In the third section of each unit, students learn about **Usage.** Subject-verb agreement, tenses, irregular verbs and word order are discussed and practiced.

The fourth section of each unit, **Proofreading**, allows students to practice the skills learned in the previous sections. The proofreading exercises teach students to find and correct errors in context.

At the end of every five units, a section **What Have You Learned?** is included. This section includes a review and a skill check. Teachers can use the review as a pre-test to determine whether students are already proficient in the skills to be taught. It also includes a spelling and usage list which can be used as either a pre- or post-test. A chart linking the review questions and the lessons in which each skill is taught enables teachers to assign specific pages instead of an entire section. Finally, this section includes a short imaginative writing exercise tied to the skills taught in the five preceding sections.

Get It Write **Right!**

Table of Contents

Units 1-10

A Spelling   B Mechanics   C Usage   D Proofreading

Get It Write **Right!**

Table of Contents

Units 11-20

A Spelling   **B** Mechanics   **C** Usage   **D** Proofreading

Get It Write **Right!**

Table of Contents

Units 21-25

A Spelling   **B** Mechanics   **C** Usage   **D** Proofreading

Get It Write **Right!**

Spell It Right!

High Frequency Words

Fill in the blank with the correct word.

1. The hat of _____ boy was red.
   a. th   b. the   c. thi   d. nose

2. He lost _____ hat at school.
   a. ear   b. is   c. his   d. hir

3. The boy _____ very sad.
   a. was   b. wuz   c. arm   d. wiz

4. He liked _____ hat.
   a. leg   b. that   c. tat   d. thit

Write It Right!

Periods and Question Marks

End each statement with a period and each question with a question mark.

Put the correct punctuation mark at the end of each sentence.

1. Cows eat hay

2. Do you eat hay

3. Are you a cow

4. Cows also like grass

5. Do you eat watermelons

Use the Right Word!

Subject-Verb Agreement

Verbs are action words. Some verbs change spelling when they change partners. I run. He runs. The word **run** is a verb.

Fill in the blank with the correct verb.

1. We _____ in caves.
       a. sleep   b. sleeps

2. We _____ bugs.
       a. eats   b. eat

3. We _____ very fast.
       a. flies   b. fly

4. We _____ not tigers.
       a. is   b. are

Draw a line from each word to its partner.

I	jumps
you	jump
she	jump

Make It Right!

Always check your spelling and punctuation after you finish writing.

Correct one mistake in each sentence.

1. My dog look at me.

2. Do you want dinner

3. Hs dish is full.

4. He does not likes his food.

5. He want ice cream.

Spell It Right!

Wh- Question Words

Wh- words like **who**, **when**, and **which** often start questions.

Fill in the blank with the correct word.

1. _____ snack do you like?
   - a. Wat
   - b. Wet
   - c. What
   - d. Wonka

2. _____ likes cookies?
   - a. Hoo
   - b. Whoo
   - c. Honk
   - d. Who

3. _____ is milk so good for you?
   - a. Y
   - b. Why
   - c. Wuzzle
   - d. Wy

4. _____ do you eat dinner?
   - a. Whan
   - b. Wen
   - c. Snort
   - d. When

5. _____ did you hide the candy?
   - a. Wear
   - b. Ware
   - c. Wher
   - d. Where

Write It Right!

Always capitalize the first word in a sentence. Capitalize the word I, and capitalize the name of a person.

Correct two mistakes in each sentence.

1. my friend, hal, is taller than my sister.

2. My sister, jan, is taller than i am.

3. my cat is shorter than my dog, jack.

4. jack is also taller than harry, my hermit crab.

Underline the words that should start with a capital letter.

john   banana   i   friend   hotdog

hat   mary   you   ben   camel

Use the Right Word!

Subject-Verb Agreement

Some action words (verbs) change spelling when they change partners.
She **eats**. We **eat**.

Fill in the blank with the correct word.

1. After school, _____ goes home.
   a. we   b. I   c. he   d. they

2. _____ likes to run all the way.
   a. They   b. I   c. We   d. He

3. _____ stay with my friend.
   a. He   b. I   c. She   d. It

4. _____ have popcorn.
   a. It   b. We   c. He   d. She

Draw a line from each word to its partner.

I   are

you   am

he   is

Make It Right!

Look very carefully to find tiny mistakes. Beware of punctuation marks and letters that are left out.

Correct two mistakes in each sentence.

1. who sent me this gift.

2. It are tied with a red ribbon

3. Wat do you think is in the box.

4. Win I open it, i will know.

Spell It Right!

Short Vowel Words

Underline the correct word.

1. A monster lives under my (bid, bad, bed).

2. He has (fazz, fuzz, fozz) on his ears.

3. He eats smelly (sicks, socks, sucks).

4. He sleeps on a pile of (dust, dist, dost).

5. He (hilps, hulps, helps) me clean my room.

Write three words starting with wh- that often ask questions.

_____   _____   _____

Write It Right!

More Capitalization

Capitalize the names of days **(Monday)** and months **(June)**.

Underline the words that should start with a capital letter.

1. Today is friday, february 1.

2. In february, we play in the snow.

3. Next wednesday, I am going skating.

4. I really like july 4.

5. the fireworks are a lot of fun.

Fill in the blanks.

Always capitalize the names of _____ and

_____.

Use the Right Word!

The words **to**, **too**, and **two** sound alike but they have different meanings. **To** is a direction word (**to** school). **Too** means "also" (He is coming **too**), or "very" (It is **too** hot). **Two** is the name of the number (I have **two** cats).

Write the correct word in the blank.

1. Jon and I are going _____ the ice cream store.

2. We will buy _____ ice cream cones.

3. Each cone will have _____ scoops.

4. I like mint chip, and Jon does _____.

5. _____ scoops melt _____ fast.

6. Pat will walk _____ the store with the _____ of us.

Make It Right!

Look very carefully to find tiny mistakes. Beware of punctuation marks and letters that are left out.

Correct two mistakes in each sentence.

1. I have to pets

2. I got my dog in june and my snake last tuesday.

3. Wat do you think my snake eats.

4. She eat mice and rats to.

5. Her name is sally

6. my dog's name si Harry.

Spell It Right!

Long Vowel Words

Choose the correct word to fill in the blank.

1. I _____ to eat tacos.
     a. luke   b. like   c. loke   d. lick

2. I put on lots of _____.
     a. chiz   b. chase   c. cheese   d. chez

3. The _____ is the best part.
     a. meat   b. met   c. mite   d. mut

4. I eat black _____ often.
     a. bens   b. bunes   c. bins   d. beans

5. My mom _____ the best tacos.
     a. maks   b. makes   c. mekes   d. miaks

Write It Right!

Use commas between the day, the date, and the year (Tuesday, April 3, 2001).
Use a comma between the town and the state in an address (Trenton, New Jersey).

Add commas where they are needed.

1. I was born on Monday January 1 1995.

2. I live in Hollywood California.

3. My father was born in London England.

4. I will visit Spain on Tuesday February 28.

5. In Rome Italy, they make yummy pizza.

Use the Right Word!

Present and Past Tense

The way words are spelled tells us whether an action is taking place now (**I jump**) or in the past (**I jumped**). Actions taking place in the past are in the past tense. To form the past tense of most action words, add **–ed**.

Change the spelling of the word in boldface to the past tense.

1. Last night I **smell** _____ something funny.

2. I almost **walk** _____ on it.

3. I **look** _____ at the floor.

4. I **lean** _____ over to see what it was.

5. I **jump** _____ out of my skin when I saw what it was.

6. I **want** _____ to run away.

Make It Right!

Look very carefully to find tiny mistakes. Beware of punctuation marks and letters that are left out.

Correct two mistakes in each sentence.

1. My birthday is saturday November 1.

2. I want to presents for my birthday

3. I hop I will get a red bik.

4. Last year, I want a new gam.

5. Wat do you want for your birthday.

Spell It Right!

Underline the correctly spelled color words.

greene	grene	green	grean
yelow	yellow	yello	yellew
black	blac	blak	block
purpl	perple	puple	purple
wite	white	whitte	witte
ornge	orage	orange	orang
brone	brown	bown	brawn

Write It Right!

Use commas in a list of three or more items. We need **eggs**, **bread**, and **milk**.
No comma is needed between two items. We need **eggs** and **bread**.

Add commas where needed. Write OK if no commas are needed.

1. I take care of my dog my cat and my fish.

2. My pets' names are Bongo Jelly and Finny.

3. Tara Amber and Pete have pets too.

4. My dog and cat are a lot of work.

5. I brush my cat walk my dog and feed my fish.

Fill in the blank

Use commas in a list of _____ or more.

Use the Right Word!

Blue, Blew, Red, Read

Blue is a color word. **Blew** sounds the same but is the past tense of blow. **Red** is a color word. **Read** sounds the same but is the past tense of read.

Words that sound the same but have different meanings when they are spelled differently are called **homonyms**.

Fill in the blank with the correct word.

1. I _____ my nose hard.

2. My nose was very _____.

3. My dad _____ to me when I was sick.

4. My toes were so cold they turned _____.

5. Our flag is _____, white, and _____.

Make It Right!

Look very carefully to find tiny mistakes. Beware of punctuation marks and letters that are left out.

Correct **two** mistakes in each sentence.

1. Her new dress is grene yellow, and blue.

2. Yesterday, the wind blowed hard

3. I red to books last month.

4. My pet snak has yellow stripes and spots.

5. The snow is wite in Fairbanks Alaska.

What Have You Learned?

Choose the correctly spelled word.

1. a. when   b. whin   c. wen   d. whan

2. a. lak   b. lach   c. lake   d. laek

3. a. orng   b. orage   c. orang   d. orange

Underline the part of the sentence with the mistake. If there is no mistake write OK.

4. Do you | like to go to | the movies.

5. School | starts | monday.

6. He | comes from | London England.

7. Joe Jim, and Jose | will come | tonight.

Choose the right word.

8. My dog _____ bones.
   a. eat   b. eats   c. eated

9. He likes his puppy chow _____.
   a. to   b. two   c. too

10. My hat _____ off in the wind.
   a. blue   b. blew   c. blowed

Correct two errors.

My dog roll in green slime

What Have You Learned?

Choose the correctly spelled word.

1. a. wat   b. what   c. wath

2. a. rin   b. runn   c. run

3. a. brown   b. bron   c. browne

Underline the part of the sentence with the mistake. If there is no mistake, write Ok.

4. My friend jill | has | a cold.

5. Will | Fred and Dave | come to?

6. Thanksgiving | is next | thursday.

7. I | live in | Portland Maine.

Choose the right word.

8. Today, I _____ feeling very happy.
   a. are   b. am   c. is

9. He _____ to get a pony.
   a. hopes   b. hops   c. hope

10. She _____ a book about dinosaurs to the class.
    a. red   b. readed   c. read

Correct two errors.

Do you like to bak cookies

What Have You Learned?

Write a sentence that is a question.

_____

_____

Write a sentence that tells the date you were born.

_____

_____

Write a sentence that uses three color words.

_____

_____

_____

Spelling and Usage List 1-5

Spelling List 1–5

the	what	bed	like	green
his	who	fuzz	cheese	yellow
was	why	socks	meat	black
that	when	dust	beans	purple
	where	helps	makes	white
				orange
				brown

Usage List 1–5

sleep	he goes	to	smell	blue
sleeps	he likes	too	smelled	blew
eats	I stay	two	walk	red
eat	we have		walked	read
fly	I am		look	
flies	you are		looked	
is	he is		lean	
are			leaned	
jump			jump	
jumps			jumped	
			want	
			wanted	

Review		Skill Check	
Question	Unit Practice	Question	Unit Practice
1	2A	1	2A
2	4A	2	3A
3	5A	3	5A
4	1B	4	2B
5	3B	5	3C
6	4B	6	3B
7	5B	7	4B
8	1C, 2C	8	1C, 2C
9	3C	9	4A, 1C, 2C
10	5C	10	5C
PR	4C, 1B	PR	4A, 1B

Get It Write **Right!**

Spell It Right!

Consonant Blend Words

Fill in the blank with the correct word.

1. I made a _____ space ship.
   a. samal   b. small   c. snall   d. smell

2. I will send it into _____ after I have lunch.
   a. slace   b. space   c. skunk   d. price

3. I hope it won't _____ up!
   a. brow   b. blow   c. bow   d. bowl

4. I am sending a _____ into space in my ship.
   a. skunk   b. skuk   c. sunk   d. slunk

5. Then space will _____ bad.
   a. sell   b. smell   c. small   d. spell

Write It Right!

More Periods and Question Marks

End each statement with a period and each question with a question mark.

Correct the punctuation mistakes in the following.

1. Some kids like to play in the dark

2. Are you afraid of the dark.

3. I play hide and seek outside at night?

4. My friend Joe likes to use a flashlight

5. If you are afraid of the dark, does a flashlight help.

Usage

Use the Right Word!

More Subject-Verb Agreement

Action words (verbs) change spelling when they change partners.
I **sit**. She **sits**.

Fill in the blank with the correct word.

1. I _____ odd things at times.
    a. sees   b. see

2. Jan never _____ what I see.
    a. sees   b. see

3. She does not _____ up in time.
    a. looks   b. look

4. She didn't _____ the flying pig.
    a. sees   b. see

Fill in the blank

An action word is called a _____.

Make It Right!

Always check your spelling and punctuation after you finish writing.

*Correct **one** mistake in each sentence.*

1. Do you know how to swim.

2. I am scared to siwm.

3. My father swim very fast.

4. Does a shark swim faster.

5. A sunburn makes my skin read.

Spelling
Mechanics
Usage
Proofreading

Spell It Right!

High Frequency Words

Fill in the blank with the correct word.

1. Summer is _____!
      a. grat   b. great   c. geat   d. python

2. _____ day is exciting.
      a. eek   b.eech   c. each   d. honk

3. Many _____ go on trips in the summer.
      a. peeple   b. python   c. people   d. peaple

4. I can stay up late _____ there is no school.
      a. python   b. becuz   c. becuase   d. because

5. I go to bed _____ nine and ten.
      a. betwen   b. beteen   c. snort   d. between

Mechanics

Spelling

Usage Proofreading

Write It Right!

Capitalize titles in a person's name. Then put a period after the title. Write **Dr.** Chen, **Mrs**. Jones, **Mr.** Smith, or **Ms.** Mendez.

Correct the mistakes in each sentence.

1. My teacher, mr chen, is very tall.

2. My doctor, dr white, is quite fat.

3. Mrs cruz has long ears.

4. Ms Smoot is very pretty.

Add capitals and periods where needed.

mr	james	dr	you
i	ms	mrs	python

Use the Right Word!

More Subject-Verb Agreement

Fill in the blank with the correct word.

1. In the spring, the flowers and grass _____.
   a. grows   b. grow

2. _____ get hay fever .
   a. He   b. I

3. Sneezing all day _____ no fun.
   a. are   b. is

4. The birds like spring more than I _____.
   a. does   b. do

5. An action word is called a _____.
   a. rhinoceros   b. verb

Draw a line from each word to its partner.

they   am

I   are

she   is

Make It Right!

Look very carefully to find tiny mistakes. Beware of punctuation marks and letters that are left out.

Correct **two** mistakes in each sentence.

1. My dentist, Dr tooth, is a silly woman.

2. She make a face when she look at my teeth.

3. A big smile of clean, wite teth is pretty.

4. Blush your teeth to times a day to keep them clean.

Spell It Right!

More Consonant Blend Words

Underline the correct word.

1. If you (bleak, break, beak) a mirror, you get 7 years bad luck.

2. Don't let a black cat (cross, closs, coss) your path.

3. Never (wak, walk, wack) under a ladder.

4. (Sep, Step, Slep) on a crack; break your mother's back.

5. Anyone who believes this (suff, stuff, slaff) is silly.

Write It Right!

Someone forgot all the commas. Add them where needed.

1. I have a drink a sandwich and a plum for lunch.

2. I was born January 1 1992.

3. I live in Trenton New Jersey

4. Vacation starts on Thursday June 20.

5. My favorite vegetables are peas beans and corn.

Use the Right Word!

Many verbs in the past tense end in **–ed** (jumped). Those verbs are called **regular verbs**. Verbs with a past tense that don't follow this spelling pattern are called **irregular verbs**.

_____

*Change the spelling of the irregular verb in **boldface** to the past tense.*

1. Last night I **go**_____ to the video store.

2. My family **see** _____ a great movie.

3. I **have**_____ popcorn and a drink.

4. The tape **break** _____ in the middle.

5. We **are** _____ upset.

6. We **take** _____ it back to the video store.

7. We **get** _____ a different one.

Make It Right!

Look very carefully to find tiny mistakes. Beware of punctuation marks and letters that are left out.

*Correct **two** mistakes in each sentence.*

1. Yesterday, I go too the zoo.

2. I saw the lions elephants and bears.

3. The elephants was spraying water with their tunks.

4. One elephant sprayed mr. lopez.

5. His clothes was soaked

6. Do you thik the elephants were laughing.

Spell It Right!

High Frequency Words

Choose the correct word to fill in the blank.

1. Going _____ a slide is sometimes scary.
   a. don   b. down   c. duwn   d. doodle

2. We have a very long slide at _____.
   a. shool   b. scool   c. school   d. salami

3. My little sister looks very _____ when she is at the top.
   a. smell   b. snort   c. smal   d. small

4. I'd like to have a pool of _____ at the bottom.
   a. watr   b. watar   c. walrus   d. water

5. Then we _____ make a big splash.
   a. cool   b. could   c. cuold   d. clod

*Hint: One way to remember the spelling of words like the answer of #5 is

Oh **U** **L**ucky **D**uck!

Write It Right!

Punctuation Practice

*Oops! Someone forgot all the punctuation marks. Add **four** commas, **five** periods and **one** question mark.*

Ms Jenkins was born in Paris France on January 1 1974   She is a

great teacher We have French cakes cookies and bread in class

sometimes Have you ever had them They are yummy

Use the Right Word!

Words must be in the right order. We say **The girl skipped** not **The skipped girl**.

Change the order of the words to make the sentence correct.

1. Boobies are odd very birds.

2. Some boobies bright blue feet have.

3. When a boy booby wants to off show, he lifts his feet.

4. Girl boobies like the boys the with bright blue feet.

5. Blue-footed boobies very are proud of their silly feet.

6. Their feet don't silly look to other boobies.

Make It Right!

Look very carefully to find tiny mistakes. Beware of punctuation marks and letters that are left out.

*Correct **two** mistakes in each sentence.*

1. Mrs Kim is my soccer coach

2. Year this, we cuold be champs.

.

3. We are working on dribbling shooting and heading the ball.

4. We meet at my schol and play games at the high schol.

5. We wil win our next gam

Spelling
Mechanics
Usage
Proofreading

Spell It Right!

Color Crossword

Across

2. The color of Rudolph's nose

5. Rhymes with burple

6. The color of clean snow

Down

1. Don't eat this color snow!

3. The color of dirt

4. The color of the sky

Write It Right!

Capitalization and Punctuation

Sentences without correct punctuation and capitalization are very hard to read.

Someone forgot all the capital letters, periods and commas. Put in 9 capital letters, 4 commas, and 6 periods. Don't forget to capitalize the names of places.

dr doomsday was born in fritz germany on october 13 1945 he is

very ugly cruel and sneaky he plans to blow up the world we have

our own secret weapon he is a superhero

Use the Right Word!

Words must be in the correct order. We say **"Joe and I are going"** not **"Me and Joe are going."** We say **"Give the ball to Jess and me"** not **"Give the ball to me and Jess."** **I** and **me** always come after any other names.

Correct the following sentences.

1. Me and Jen are best friends.

2. My mom gave ice cream to me and my brother.

3. Me and Sarah like to build things.

4. Joe, me, and Jack play computer games.

5. Computer monsters get me, Ryan, and Emma all the time.

Underline the word that makes the correct rule.

I or me always comes (before, after) any other names.

Make It Right!

Look very carefully to find tiny mistakes. Beware of punctuation marks and letters that are left out.

Correct two mistakes in each sentence.

1. Should me and Jill go with Brad.

2. They painted my schol yallow.

3. Juan is grumby and sad yesterday.

4. Dr Jones wears a wite coat.

5. The falling bricks coud hurt me and Jake.

What Have You Learned?

Choose the correctly spelled word.

1. a. poeple   b. peeple   c. people

2. a. betwen   b. between   c. betwean

3. a. coud   b. cuold   c. could

Underline the part of the sentence with the mistake. If there is no mistake, write OK.

4. Do Lisa and I | get to go | too.

5. His grandfather | was born on | December 31 1940.

6. Dr Dog | is the name | of my vet.

7. Me, Will, and Ben | went | to the movie.

Choose the right word.

8 I _____ feeling happy.
     a. is   b. am   c. were

9. Yesterday, he _____ a cold.
     a. had   b. has   c. having

10. Last night, we_____ to a movie.
     a. goed   b. go   c. went

Correct two errors.

Mrs. smith, the nurse, gave me and my brother a shot.

Skill Check 6-10

What Have You Learned?

Choose the correctly spelled word.

1. a. because   b. becuase   c. becase

2. a. wak   b. walk   c. wolk

3. a. perple   b. purpel   c. purple

Underline the part of the sentence with the mistake. If there is no mistake, write OK.

4. My friend's father, | mr. Perkins, | is very tall.

5. Are you | afraid | of the dark?

6. We are coming | to visit you on | Thursday February 1.

7. Give the extra | popcorn to | me, Jon, and Bess.

Choose the right word.

8. Brad_____ a ghost last night.
    a. sees   b. seed   c. saw

9. Now he _____ a stuffy nose.
    a. had   b. has   c. haves

10. A raccoon lives _____ by the creek.
    a. don   b. down   c. doun

Correct two errors.

In Flagstaff Arizona, it is to cold to go outside today.

What Have You Learned?

Address a letter to your teacher. Your teacher lives at 65 Looney Lane in your town. He or she has the same zip code as you do. Don't forget to add punctuation where necessary.

Your name _____

Your street address _____

Your city, state zip code

                      Your teacher's name _____

                      Your teacher's street address _____

                      Your teacher's city, state zip code

_____

_____

_____

                    _____

                    _____

                    _____

Spelling and Usage List 6-10

Spelling List 6-10

small	great	break	down	red
space	each	cross	school	purple
blow	people	walk	small	white
skunk	because	step	water	yellow
smell	between	stuff	could	brown
				blue

Usage List 6-10

see	they grow	went
sees	I get	saw
looks	it is	had
look	I do	broke
	they are	were
	I am	took
	she is	got

Review		Skill Check	
Question	Unit Practice	Question	Unit Practice
1	7A	1	7A
2	7A	2	8A
3	9A	3	5A, 10A
4	1B, 6B	4	7B
5	4B	5	
6	7B	6	4B
7	10C	7	10C
8	1C, 2C, 7C	8	8C
9	8C	9	8C
10	8C	10	9A
PR	2B, 7B, 10C	PR	4B, 3C

Get It Write **Right!**

Spell It Right!

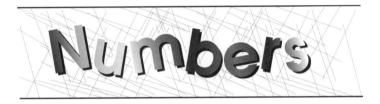

Fill in the blank with the correct number word.

1. _____ How many days are in a week?

2. _____ How many days are in a weekend?

3. _____ How many sides does a square have?

4. _____ How many wheels are on a tricycle?

5. _____ How many lives does a cat have?

6. _____ How many people are you if you are alone?

7. _____ What number word rhymes with "hate"?

8. _____ How old are you when you are born?

Write It Right!

Dear Uncle Sam

Use a comma after the greeting in a letter. Use a comma after the closing of a letter. Sign your name on the line below the closing.

> Dear Mom and Dad,
>
> Blah, blah, blah.
>
> Love,
>
> Jimmy

_____

Add correct punctuation to each letter and then sign the name of the person who wrote the letter.

Dear Bad Guys

Please return my web shooter.

Sincerely yours

_____

Dear Mr Hanson

Can you repair my cape My tights are shrinking, and it is hard to put them on in a telephone booth. I think I need a bigger size

Regards

_____

Use the Right Word!

Which is Witch?

Which and **witch** are **homonyms**—words that sound the same but have different meanings when they are spelled differently. **Which** is a word that starts a question. **Witch** describes an old hag who rides a broom.

Find the word in each sentence that is spelled wrong. Replace it with a word that sounds the same but is spelled differently.

1. Fluffy has won nose.

2. Above her nose, Fluffy has too eyes.

3. I bet you guessed that Fluffy has for feet.

4. You no that Fluffy is an animal.

5. Fluffy is not the boa constrictor that eight those rats.

Make It Right!

Little Red Riding Hood wrote this letter to her grandma but forgot all the punctuation. Help her out by adding six commas, two periods and two question marks.

6 Forest Lane

Woody Lake Michigan

July 9 2005

Dear Grandma

May I visit you next week   I want to walk over to your house on

Saturday   My mom says that the woods are scary   Have you seen

any bears lions or tigers

Love

Little Red RH

Spell It Right!

High Frequency Words

Choose the correct word to fill in the blank.

1. Learning how to tie shoelaces is difficult for little _____.
   a. brooms   b. childs   c. childran   d. children

2. One lace goes _____ the loop.
   a. arond   b. spider   c. around   d. aruond

3. Then it goes _____ the hole.
   a. threw   b. though   c. through   d. snork

4. People use _____ ways to teach kids.
   a. different   b. differant   c. donkey   d. diferant

5. When they mess up the knot, they have to tie it _____.
   a. agin   b. again   c. agen   d. aardvark

Write It Right!

Complete Sentences

A sentence must express a complete idea. It must have a subject and a predicate containing a verb. The subject is something that acts, and the predicate contains action.

Make your own complete sentences. **Draw a line** *from each* **subject** *in the first column to a* **predicate** *in the second column. Try to make a story.*

1. Jean and the elephant   was hot.

2. The elephant   like to play hide and seek.

3. The other kids   runs really fast.

4. Usually, the winner   was hard to hide.

5. The afternoon   could find them easily.

Use the Right word!

Words that sound the same but have different meanings when they are spelled differently are called **homonyms**. The words **bee** and **be** are homonyms.

_____

Fill in the blanks with homonyms. The words in parentheses are hints.

1. A _____ (an insect) sting won't _____ too painful.

2. The dinner _____(time unit) at _____ house is 6 p.m.

3. You should _____ (purchase) the pants _____

   (next to) those shirts.

4. He found the _____ (complete) dinosaur skeleton in

   the _____.

5. I _____ (mailed) a letter using one_____ stamps.

Make It Right!

Fix the errors in the letter below. Add three commas; fix four spelling errors, and complete an incomplete sentence.

July 6 2002

Dear Mom and Dad

Camp is really fun. We run aruond all night. At the campfire, I ate about for hundred marshmallows. Had a bellyache. We have lots of diferent things too do here.

Love

Taylor

Spelling

Mechanics

Usage   Proofreading

Spell It Right!

A **contraction** is two words smashed together with one or more letters left out and replaced by an apostrophe. The contraction of **cannot** is **can't**. Can you tell which letters are replaced by the apostrophe?

Choose the correct spelling of the contraction.

1. are not
   a. are'not   b. ar'nt   c. arent   d. aren't

2. it is
   a. i'ts   b. it's   c. itsy bitsy   d. it'is

3. should not
   a. shouldn't   b. shouldy   c. should't   d. should'not

4. would have
   a. woody   b. would've   c. wouldve   d. wouldh've

5. will not
   a. willn't   b. won't   c. willnt   c. willy wonka
   (Watch out! This tricky one doesn't follow the rule.)

Mechanics

Spelling

Usage | Proofreading

Write It Right!

Exclamations!

Use an exclamation mark at the end of a forceful command (**Go home!**), an exclamation (**Wow!**), or sentence that needs emphasis (**I'm starved!**). Using an exclamation point is almost like yelling.

Choose the correct punctuation (exclamation point, question mark, or period) for each sentence below.

1. Did you see something move

2. Maybe it was a ghost

3. Eeeek

4. Are you scared

5. Is it in the closet

6. Help

7. Run for your life

8. I'm going to open the door

9. It's only my kitty

Use the Right Word!

Action words (verbs) change depending on whether the action occurs in the present, the past, or the future. I **jump**; I **jumped**; I will **jump**.

Fill in the chart with the correct verb tense form.

Present Tense	Past Tense	Future Tense
kick		will kick
	worked	
climb		
		will thump
	spooked	

Make It Right!

Correct the errors in the sentences below. Find two punctuation errors and three spelling errors.

Yikes. The ground is shaking. Have you ever felt an earthquake. If

you feel an earthquake, you should'nt run outside. You should

stand in a doorway or sit under a table so things wont fall on you. It

will be over in to minutes.

Spell It Right!

Verb Endings

To form the past tense of most verbs, add **–ed** (climb, climb**ed**). If the verb ends in silent **–e**, drop the silent **–e** and add **-ed**.

Write the past tense form of the verbs below.

1. paint _____

2. hope _____

3. crack _____

4. jump _____

5. race _____

6. look _____

7. snoop _____

8. free _____

9. snarl _____

10. replace _____

Write It Right!

More Complete Sentences

A **sentence** must express a complete idea. It must have a **subject** (something that acts or appears) and a **predicate** (an action or an appearance).

Each sentence part below is missing either a subject or a predicate. Fill in the blank with the name of the part in parentheses. Then complete the sentence adding the missing part.

1. <u>Subject</u>_____ (the large foolish mole)

2. _____ (digs tunnels in the pasture)

3. _____ (pokes his head out to look at the sky)

4. _____ (his underground home)

Choose the correct word to fill in the blank.

5. The predicate contains a word called a _____.
     a. noun   b. verb

6. The subject contains a person, place or thing which is usually

     a _____.
     a. noun   b. verb

Use the Right Word!

To change most verbs from present to past tense you add **-ed**. (I **jump**, I **jumped**).   Verbs that do not follow this pattern are called irregular verbs.

Fill in the chart with the correct spelling of the irregular verb using I as the subject.

Present Tense	Past Tense
eat	
	had
know	
sit	
drink	
	came
	spoke

Make It Right!

In the following letter, correct four spelling errors and one incomplete sentence. Add two commas and two periods.

3 Forest Lane

Woodland PA

May 3, 2005

Dear Mr and Mrs Bear,

Im sorry I goed into your house and eated your porridge. I didn't

know that the chair would break when I sitted in it. I cried all last

night. Want to say how sorry I am.

Regretfully

Goldilocks

Spelling

Mechanics

Usage

Proofreading

Spell It Right!

High Frequency Words

Correct the spelling of each underlined word.

1. The <u>hi</u> diving board is scary.

2. The low board is <u>hi</u> <u>enuff</u> for me.

3. <u>Wile</u> I climbed the ladder, I wondered if I would have the courage to jump.

4. I <u>thught</u> I could do it.

5. <u>Shoold</u> I close my eyes, or <u>shood</u> I jump with them open?

6. Maybe I <u>shuld</u> forget the <u>hole</u> thing!

Hint: Did you remember **O**h **U** **l**ucky **d**uck?

Write It Right!

Capitalizing Holidays

Capitalize the names of holidays (**Christmas**). The names of seasons (**spring**) are lower case.

Correct the capitalization in the following sentences.

1. My favorite holiday is halloween.

2. My mother likes mother's day the best.

3. Mother's day is the second sunday in may.

4. Our fourth of july parade is usually quite lively.

5. Spring is my favorite season, but Andy likes Fall the best.

6. This Winter, christmas falls on the last friday in december.

Use the Right Word!

More Irregular Verbs

Change the boldfaced verb to the tense in parentheses.

1. Yesterday, a horse **give** (past tense) _____me a kick in the behind.

2. I **fell** (present tense) _____down quite often when it is icy.

3. She **sings** (past tense) _____ a lullaby to the baby.

4. Last week, he **is** (past tense) _____ sick.

5. Sometimes her boyfriend **brought** (present tense) _____ her flowers.

6. She **says** (past tense) _____she **is** _____ (past tense) embarrassed.

Make It Right!

In the following letter, correct three spelling errors and one incomplete sentence. Add two commas and one exclamation point. Correct the capitalization on three words.

August 16, 2005

Dear Aunt Jenny

Thank you very much for the new game you sent on memorial day.

It is so cool.   It shuold keep me busy all summer. I thuoght I new

how to play it, but I was wrong. Is difficult.

I hope you are having a fun Summer.

Love

Marcie

What Have You Learned?

*Check the spelling of the **underlined** words. Correct if necessary.*

1. The naughty puppy ate <u>to</u> steaks and <u>eight</u> hamburgers.

2. My brother is <u>scared</u> of <u>bes</u> and other insects.

3. That <u>should</u> be <u>enuff</u>.

4. I <u>jumped</u> over the rocks and <u>sitted</u> down.

5. I <u>thought</u> he <u>speaked</u> and <u>singed</u> well.

Check if the following are complete sentences. If incomplete, add words to correct. If complete, write OK.

6. Ran to the store. _____

7. A huge red balloon. _____

8. The wolf howled. _____

Correct the following letter. Fix four punctuation errors, one capitalization error and four spelling errors.

June 6 2005

Dear sir

I cent away for the action figure advertised on your cereal box.

You sayed it was life sized, but it wasnt even three inches hi. I am so

angry. I want my money back.

Sincerely

Thomas

What Have You Learned?

Check the spelling of the underlined words. Correct if necessary.

1. <u>Seven</u> <u>diferent</u> <u>childrin</u> asked me that question.

2. I <u>thought</u> I <u>new</u> how to find the answer.

3. <u>Wile</u> everyone slept, I <u>looked</u> the <u>hole</u> night for it.

4. I <u>could'nt</u> find <u>one</u> hint.

Check if the following are complete sentences. If incomplete, add words to correct. If complete, write OK.

5. My friend with the red hair. _____

6. She swam like a fish. _____

7. Was a shark. _____

Correct the following letter. Fix five punctuation errors, two capitalization errors and three spelling errors.

October 12, 2005

Dear Mr Mendez

I am making a haunted house in my garage for halloween.   I will

need to rent to mummies and thre skeletons. It will be scary Last

Spring, you sayed you would help me. Is the offer still good.

Sincerely yours

Madison

Get It Write **Right!**

What Have You Learned?

Your favorite uncle is a nutty zoo keeper. He has offered to send you a tiger cub for your birthday. Write him a polite letter explaining why you can't keep a tiger cub as a pet.

_____ (your street address)

_____ (your town, state and zip code)

_____ (the date)

Dear Uncle _____ (your uncle's name)

_____

_____

_____

_____

_____

_____ (the closing)

_____ (your name)

Spelling and Usage List 11-15

Spelling List 11-15

seven	children	aren't	painted	high
two	around	it's	hoped	enough
four	through	shouldn't	cracked	while
three	different	would've	jumped	thought
nine	again	won't	raced	should
one			looked	whole
eight			snooped	
zero			freed	
			snarled	
			replaced	

Usage List 11-15

one	bee	kicked	eat	give
won	be	work	ate	gave
two	hour	will work	have	fall
too	our	climbed	had	fell
four	buy	will climb	know	sing
for	by	thump	knew	sang
know	whole	thymped	sit	is
no	hole	spook	sat	was
ate	sent	will spook	drink	bring
eight	cent		drank	bring
			come	says
			came	said
			speak	
			spoke	

Review		Skill Check	
Question	Unit Practice	Question	Unit Practice
1	3C, 11A, 11C	1	11A, 12A
2	12C	2	15A, 14C
3	15A	3	15A, 14A, 12C
4	14A, 14C	4	13A, 11A
5	14C, 15C	5	12B, 14B
6	12B, 14B	6	12B, 14B
7	12B, 14B	7	12B, 14B
8	12B, 14B		
PR	4B, 7B, 12C, 15C, 13A, 15A, 13B, 11B	PR	7B, 11B, 15B. 11C, 11A, 13B, 15C

Get It Write Right!

Spell It Right!

Compound Words

Compound words are formed by squashing together two smaller words. **Handstand** is formed by mashing together **hand** and **stand**. Don't leave out any letters!

Fill in the blank with a compound word made from two little words in the same sentence.

1. **Row** this **boat** over to that _____**rowboat**_____.

2. My dad says "Time for bed," when it is my _____.

3. My dog stole a _____ from the hot grill.

4. The worker had to plow through the snow to get to the

_____.

5. Road signs are high way above the _____.

6. That road going down toward town takes you to

_____.

Write It Right!

ABCDEFGHIJKLMNOPQRSTUVWXYZ

To arrange words in alphabetical order, look at the first letter of each word. Put a word starting with **a** first, **b** second and so forth: **ant**, **bear**, **zebra**.

Arrange this class list in alphabetical order. Juan, Bob, Cathy, Teddy.

1. _____

2. _____

3. _____

4. _____

Mr. Bison, Mrs. Aardvark, Miss Wombat, Ms. Kangaroo, Mr. Zebra are listed in the zoo phone book in alphabetical order.

1. Whose name is first? _____

2. Whose name is last? _____

3. Who comes after Mr. Bison? _____

4. Who comes before Mr. Zebra? _____

To sort words into alphabetical order, you must know the alphabet by heart. Do you know the alphabet song?

Use the Right Word!

Homonyms are words that sound the same but have different meanings depending on their spelling. **Know** and **no** are homonyms.

Fill in the blank with a homonym of another word in the sentence.

1. I **know** there is _____ *no* _____ pie left.

2. In the distance, I can see the _____.

3. The _____ skin rug feels soft against my bare skin.

4. After you get the milk, meet me at the _____ counter.

5. I love the tall tale about why the pig has a curly _____.

6. The music is so loud here, that I can't _____ myself

   think.

Make It Right!

Correct five spelling errors, one capitalization error, one punctuation error, and one incomplete sentence.

The Tale of a Whale

If you are lucky, you can see something odd down at the beach in january. Sometimes a huge whale will jump out of the see. His tale looks as big as a skyscraper. Makes a splash like a tidal wav.

Sometimes you can even here the noises the whales make. Do you no what they are saying.

Spell It Right!

More Compound Words

Add one of the words in the top list to each of the words below to form a compound word.

ring	band	set	boat
man	check	bow	pack

sun _____

rain _____

mail _____

watch _____

sail _____

pay _____

back _____

ear _____

Most compound words are nouns. A **noun** is a word that names a **person**, **place**, or **thing**.

Underline the nouns.

off   rope   Miami   in   doctor   very

Write It Right!

ABCDEFGHIJKLMNOPQRSTUVWXYZ

Sometimes two words start with the same letter. To arrange them in alphabetical order, look at the second letter. **Bank** is before **boat** in alphabetical order because **a** comes before **o**.

List these names in alphabetical order.

Bill   Bret   Bob   Ben   Bart

_____

_____

_____

_____

_____

If the first two letters are the same, look at the next letter to determine the order. If the next letter is the same, go to the next letter and so on.

Circle the letter in each word that helps you determine which name goes first.

Babs   Babara

Use the Right Word!

More Irregular Verbs

Put the verb in parentheses into the past tense.

1. Last year I (grow) _____ sunflowers.

2. Last month I (begin)_____ to prepare the garden.

3. I (am) _____ hard at work digging over the soil.

4. I (find) _____a rock with streaks of gold.

5. I (tell) _____ my dad.

6. "It's fool's gold," he (says) _____.

Fill in the blank.

7. An action word is called a _____.

8. A word that names a person, place, or thing is called a

_____.

Make It Right!

Choose the part of the sentence with the error.

1. My blue bacpack is | really heavy when | I fill it with books.
    a.   b.   c.

2. Last summer | I growed radishes | in my garden.
    a.   b.   c.

3. Look at | what I fuond | under my bed!
    a.   b.   c.

4. My mother | lost her favorite | earing.
    a.   b.   c.

5. A big truck | rolled over | on the hiway.
    a.   b.   c.

6. I telled my | dog not to play | with snakes.
    a.   b.   c.

7. After I got | home, I beginned | my homework.
    a.   b.   c.

8. For dinner, I ate | hotdogs corn and | baked beans.
    a.   b.   c.

Spelling

Mechanics

Usage   Proofreading

Spell It Right!

More Verb Endings

Verbs in the present tense often change spelling when the person doing the action changes. **I** jump. When **he**, **she**, or **it** is doing the action, add an **–s**. **He** jumps. Add **–es** to verbs ending in **–s**, **–sh**, **-ch**, **-x**, or **–z**.

Fill in the chart

First person present tense	Third person present tense
I run	he runs
I sniff	he
I catch	she
I smash	it
I walk	she
I kiss	he
I pass	he
I laugh	she

Write It Right!

More Complete Sentences

A complete sentence contains a subject (a person, place or thing which is acting or appearing) and a predicate (an action or appearance).

Draw a line between the subject and the predicate in the following sentences.

1. I | watch too much television these days.

2. My eyes get red and blurry.

3. The ads seem a little silly sometimes.

4. Too many people believe the ads on television.

Mark each sentence complete (C) or incomplete (I).

5. I like the Discovery Channel.

6. Lots of weird animals.

7. Often hunting prey in the jungles all over the world.

8. I would love to take pictures of wildlife.

Underline the nouns.

and   man   room   hot   giraffe

Use the Right Word!

The articles **a** and **an** mean the same. Use **a** before a word starting with a consonant or a consonant sound—**a pot**. Use **an** before a word starting with a vowel—**an apple**, or a vowel sound—**an hour**.

*Write either **a** or **an** in the blanks.*

How to Make _____ Awful Mess

First take _____ bucket of squishy mud. Mix it with _____ quart of

motor oil. Next add _____ bottle of ketchup and _____ enor-

mous squirt of mustard. Empty _____ entire jar of paste into the

bucket and add _____ helping of green slime. Cover your arms

and legs with the mixture. It will only take you _____ hour in the

tub to clean yourself off.

Did you notice that the consonant **h** in **hour** is silent and that the word starts with the vowel sound?

Make It Right!

Correct six spelling errors, one punctuation error, and one incomplete sentence.

One kid at my school is a awful bully. Every time he pass me in the hall, he laughes at me. Bosses everyone around. Sometimes at lunch he walks by the tables and smashs my sandwiches. My friend Jim never walks past him if he can avoid it. Some day, when a teacher catchs him, he is going to be in trouble? He thinks he is cool, but he is a ugly troll.

Spell It Right!

High Frequency Words

Choose the correctly spelled word to fill in the blank.

1. Choose the right _____.
   a. anser   b. answer   c. aardvark   d. anwser

2. You have _____ choices.
   a. sevarel   b. snortly   c. severel   d. several

3. This page is _____ simple.
   a. realy   b. reelly   c. really   d. rhino

4. I got a bad grade even _____ I studied.
   a. thought   b. thuogh   c. thoe   d. though

5. My _____ did the best in the class.
   a. goop   b. groop   c. gruop   d. group

6. Your painting is very _____.
   a. beatiful   b. beautiful   d. borkle   d. bueatiful

7. Next year we _____to add fractions.
   a. laern   b. lern   d. lurn   d. learn

Mechanics

Spelling

Usage

Proofreading

Write It Right!

Punctuation Review

Oops! Someone forgot most of the punctuation. Add 5 periods, 1 question mark, 1 apostrophe, and 5 commas.

34 Green Grocer Lane

Emerald City OZ 92034

June 2 2005

Dear Dr Dimwit

I am having trouble with my new brain   It doesnt seem to work very

well   I had an x-ray taken, and it looked a lot like a cabbage   Is it

supposed to look that way When I have the straw replaced next

time, please check my heart my liver, and my kidneys too

Sincerely yours

Moe Scarecrow

Fill in the blanks.

A noun is a word that names a _____, _____, or

_____.

Get It Write **Right!**

Understand the Structure

From the words below, choose the verbs and use them to fill in the table.

| hat | **ran** | balloon | wrote | **am** | over |
| froze | said | will hide | pretty | did | in |

Present Tense	Future Tense	Past Tense
run	will run	ran
am		

Make It Right!

Correct nine spelling mistakes.

Last night I had a awful dream. I was with a grupe of kids in my

classroom. I wanted to go out to recess realy badly, but the

teacher wouldn't let me go. He sayed I had to anser severel ques-

tions first. I fuond the answers in my science book, writed them

down, and runned outside, but recess was already over. What a

terrible dream!

Spell It Right!

Nouns are words that name a person, place, or thing **(Jack, Boston, ball)**. Nouns can be singular (one **bat**) or plural (**bats**--more than one bat). Usually the plural is formed by adding **–s** (one cow, two cow**s**). To form the plural of nouns ending in **s**, **sh**, **ch**, and **x** add **–es** (one fox, two fox**es**).

Change the boldfaced noun to its plural.

On the twelfth day of Christmas my true love gave to me:

twelve **cake** baking

eleven **dish** breaking

ten **glass** filling

nine **cow** chewing

eight **fox** fighting

seven **match** lighting

six **snake** squirming

five meatball **sandwich**

Write It Right!

More Alphabetical Order

Fill in the blank.

a. plum   b. apple   c. orange   d. cherry   e. raspberry

1. Which is first in alphabetical order? _____

2. Which is last? _____

3. Which comes after orange? _____

a. Jack   b. Adam   c. John   d. Bart   e. Brad

4. Which name comes after Adam? _____

5. Which name is last? _____

a. Smith   b. Jones   c. Johnson   d. Ruiz   e. Johnston

6. Which name comes first? _____

7. Which name is second? _____

8. Which name is third? _____

Use the Right Word!

More Homonyms

Find the homonym in each sentence and change it to the other word that sounds the same but has a different meaning. In the first five sentences, the homonym is in **boldface***.*

1. My friend **maid** a rowboat.

2. Instead of **would**, he made it out of cardboard.

3. Cardboard is **to** thin for a rowboat.

4. When I sat in it, I went **threw** the bottom.

5. It was muddy in **their**.

6. You **wood** think he would know better.

7. He was so silly that I **through** him in the water.

8. Then he threw me in **to**.

9. My friends, Michelle and Elise go **too** the lake sometimes.

10. **There** rowboat is better than ours.

Make It Right!

Correct seven spelling errors, one capitalization error, and one incomplete sentence.

My friend's mother, mrs. James, has a thing about cows. She has

cows on her dishs and glasses. She fills there house with cows maid

of wood and plastic. I don't think cows are so grate. I prefer foxs

and snakes myself. Imagine beutiful glasses and dishs decorated

with snakes. Big, long snakes with poisonous fangs!

What Have You Learned?

Check the spelling of the underlined words. Correct if necessary.

1. Do you <u>realy</u> <u>no</u> the <u>answer</u>?

2. She <u>catchs</u> the ball and <u>throws</u> it <u>threw</u> the grass.

3. A <u>rainbow</u> floated over the <u>hiway</u>.

4. <u>A</u> ice storm <u>freezed</u> my <u>nose</u> and toes.

Write the names in alphabetical order.

Ben   Paul   Pat

5. _____

6. _____

7. _____

Correct nine spelling errors and two punctuation errors.

Who wood believe it. My friend told me a tail so silly that I

laughed. He siad that he finded some pirate gold in a cave by the

see. Pirates hid there gold in a small would chest there. I think my

friend is watching to many movies

What Have You Learned?

Check the spelling of the underlined words. Correct if necessary.

1. Her <u>earing</u> and <u>watchband</u> are <u>maid</u> of gold.

2. The <u>foxs</u> <u>hid</u> in <u>there</u> burrow.

3. My shirt <u>matchs</u> my <u>skirt</u> and socks <u>to</u>.

4. Make up <u>a</u> <u>tale</u> about <u>a</u> ant and <u>a</u> butterfly.

Write the names in alphabetical order.

Ricky   Elmer   John   Jared

5. _____

6. _____

7. _____

8. _____

Correct eight spelling errors, one punctuation error, and one capitalization error.

Last winter was an cold one. The lake freezed, and the hiways were covered with ice. Wood spring ever come. Finally, in march, I saw a green leaf sticking threw the snow. On the first warm day, my friends throwed off there coats and hats. Spring was hear at last!

What Have You Learned?

*Oops! Whoever wrote the dictionary goofed and left out the words **snork**, **aprix**, **fizbat**, **borkle**, and **garg**. List the pretend words in alphabetical order. Label each as either a noun or a verb, and then make up a silly definition.*

aprix   noun   a large door knob with giant purple and

green spots

_____   _____   _____

_____

_____   _____   _____

_____

_____   _____   _____

_____

_____   _____   _____

_____

Spelling and Usage List 16-20

Spelling List 16–20

rowboat	sunset	runs	answer	cakes
bedtime	rainbow	sniffs	several	dishes
hotdog	mailman	catches	really	glasses
snowplow	watchband	smashes	though	cows
highway	sailboat	walks	group	foxes
downtown	paycheck	kisses	beautiful	matches
	backpack	passes	learn	snakes
	earring	laughs		sandwiches

Usage List 16–20

know	grow	a	run	maid
no	grew	an	ran	made
see	begin		write	would
sea	began		wrote	wood
meet	am		am	to
meat	was		will be	too
tale	find		was	threw
tail	found		say	through
hear	tell		said	their
here	told		hide	there
bear	says		hid	
bare	said		do	
			did	
			freeze	
			froze	

Review		Skill Check	
Question	Unit Practice	Question	Unit Practice
1	19A, 16C	1	17A, 20C
2	18A, 20C	2	20A, 19C, 20C
3	16A, 17A	3	20A, 20C
4	18C, 19C	4	18C, 16C
5	16B, 17B, 20B	5	16B, 17B, 20B
6	16B, 17B, 20B	6	16B, 17B, 20B
7	16B, 17B, 20B	7	16B, 17B, 20B
		8	16B, 17B, 20B
PR	20C, 1B, 17C, 16C, 19C	PR	18C, 19C, 16A, 1B, 3B, 20C, 16C

Get It Write **Right!**

Spell It Right!

High Frequency Words

Choose the correct words to fill in the blanks.

1. I live in the _____.
   a. united states   b. United Stups   c. United States

2. The _____to our north is Canada.
   a. countrey   b. country   c. counter

3. Mexico is in North _____.
   a. america   b. America   c. Mongolia

4. George Washington is called the _____ of our country.
   a. further   b. father   c. feather

5. I can't _____ when he lived.
   a. rememeber   b. remeber   c. remember

6. The date isn't _____.
   a. inportant   b. importent   c. important

7. His birthday is a _____.
   a. holoday   b. holiday   c. holaday

Write It Right!

Capitalize the first and last words of a book title and all the important words. Do not capitalize **and**, **the**, **a**, **of**, and **but** unless they are the first or last word. <u>Underline</u> book titles.

Correct the following sentences.

1. My favorite book is tales of a fourth grade nothing.

2. My brother's favorite is the hobbit.

3. My dad's favorite is into thin air.

4. My mom's favorite book is art through the ages.

5. My sister's favorite is freckle juice.

Use the Right Word!

More Irregular Verbs

Choose the correct past tense form of the verb.

1. My class _____ on a whale-watching trip.
   - a. goes
   - b. went
   - c. goed

2. We _____ the first whales after an hour of sailing.
   - a. see
   - b. seed
   - c. saw

3. They _____ and jumped into the air.
   - a. swam
   - b. swimmed
   - c. swim

4. Whales do not get seasick, but I _____.
   - a. do
   - b. did
   - c. doed

5. After we returned, we _____ tired.
   - a. ared
   - b. was
   - c. were

6. The next day, we _____ poems about whales.
   - a. writed
   - c. write
   - c. wrote

Fill in the blank.

To form the past tense of a regular verb ending in silent -e like fade,

add _____.

Make It Right!

Correct two punctuation errors, one book title, four irregular verbs, and one other spelling error.

When I was little, I loved books by Dr Seuss. I sitted for hours listening

to Green eggs and Ham. I remamber my dad singed it to me just

before I goed to bed. He knowed it by heart. Did you have a

favorite bedtime story.

Spell It Right!

Verbs Ending in -Y

Adding a suffix (word ending) to verbs ending in **-y** can be tricky. When adding an **-s** to a verb ending in consonant then **-y** (**cry**), change the **-y** to **-i** and add **-es** (**cries**). To change a verb ending in a consonant then **-y** from the present tense (**I cry**) to the past tense (**I cried**), change the **-y** to **-i** and add **-ed**.

Present Tense	Present Tense	Past Tense
I spy	He spies	I spied
You carry	He	I
We hurry	Bill	He
I fry	He	We
You worry	She	They
They reply	He	Marge

Write It Right!

Use quotation marks " " around the exact words someone says. Always put the period inside the quotation marks. Martin Luther King said, " I have a dream."

In the following sentences, add quotation marks and periods.

1. My mom called out, Time to go

2. She said, Get your backpack

3. She added, You have soccer practice after school

4. She nagged, Pick up those socks

5. She says the same thing every morning: Don't forget your lunch

Use the Right Word!

More Irregular Verbs

The past tense of some irregular verbs ends in **–ought** or **–aught**.

Write the past tense of the verb on the line.

1. My sister and I (buy) _____ a new CD.

2. We (bring) _____ it home to play it.

3. We (think) _____ it would be great.

4. We (fight) _____ about who would get it first.

5. Our dad (catches) _____ us arguing.

6. He (teaches) _____ us how to solve our problem.

Fill in the blank.

An action word is a part of speech called a _____.

Make It Right!

Correct four spelling errors and one book title. Add quotation marks where necessary.

I getted in big trouble with my sister yesterday. She bringed home a library book, The Land of dinosaurs, that looked really interesting. I was looking at it in the bathrom when she knocked on the door. She yelled, Hurry up, Jimmy! Then she started pounding on the door. I need to get in there!

Wait a minute, I replyed. By mistake, I dumped the book into the tub. Oh, oh!

Underline the verb

pretty   jump   of   python

Spell It Right!

Nouns Ending in -Y

Nouns name a person, place, or thing (boy, bedroom, sock). To form the plural of nouns ending in a **vowel then -y**, **add -s** (key, key**s**). To form the plural of words ending in a **consonant then -y**, change the **-y** to **-i** and add **-es** (city, cit**ies**).

Fill in the chart

Singular	Consonant then -y?	Vowel then -y?	Plural
city	yes	no	cities
donkey	no	yes	
army			
party			
day			
monkey			

Remember the rhyme: Consonant, -y, change -y to -i.

Write It Right!

Put quotation marks around the exact words someone says. Capitalize the first word of the quotation and use a comma to separate the speaker from the quotation. Comas and periods always go in front of quotation marks. Josh said, "The sky is falling." "No it isn't," said Joe.

Capitalize the first word of quotations and add commas where needed.

1. Jenna said "my dog ate my homework."

2. Bill added "my homework fell in the tub."

3. "I lost my homework on the way to school " claimed Tom.

4. "My sister lined the bird cage with my homework " complained Ella.

5. Chad said "aliens took my homework."

6. "Your excuses seem a bit silly " replied the teacher.

7. She added "I don't believe you."

Use the Right Word!

Moose, Mice, Meese?

Sometimes plurals of animal names are really strange.

Guess the correct plural form.

1. One mouse, two   mouses   meese   mice

2. One moose, two   mooses   meese   moose

3. One goose, two   geese   gooses   goose

4. One wolf, two   wolfs   wolves   wolfes

5. One sheep, two   sheeps   sheep   sheepies

6. One louse, two   louses   lice   looloos

7. One skunk, two   stinkers   smellies   skunks

8. One deer, two   dearies   deers   deer

Fill in the blank.

A word that names a person, place, or thing is called a

_____.

Make It Right!

Choose the part of the sentence with the error.

1. "I'll have │ frys with │ that," I added.
      a.   b.   c.

2. The wolfs │ caught three deer │ this week.
      a.   b.   c.

3. "Add a little │ more yellow, I │ suggested.
      a.   b.   c.

4. My friend │ replied "I │ prefer pink."
      a.   b.   c.

5. My dad cuaght │ four mice │ in the traps.
      a.   b.   c.

6. She worries │ that she won't │ remeber her number.
      a.   b.   c.

7. Armies of lice │ live on the fur of │ mooses.
      a.   b.   c.

8. He thinked │ that was a stupid │ sentence.
      a.   b.   c.

Spell It Right!

Sometimes when you add a suffix (a word ending) like **-ing** to a word like **bat**, you must double the final consonant—**batting**. You double the final consonant if all of the following are true: if the suffix begins with a vowel, if the root word is one syllable, and if the root has one short vowel followed by one consonant.

_____

Fill in the chart.

Root word	Suffix	Suffix begins with a vowel?	One syllable root?	One short vowel?	One final consonant?	Double the consonant?
bat	-ed	yes	yes	yes	yes	yes
ship	-ment					
shut	-ing					
center	-ed					
tap	-ing					
snob	-ish					
hop	-ed					
peak	-ing					
jump	-ed					

Write each word with its suffix.

_____   _____   _____

_____   _____   _____

_____   _____   _____

Write It Right!

Indirect Quotations

The exact words a person says are called direct quotations. **Mom yelled, "Get to bed!"** When a person reports the main idea but not the exact words, quotations are indirect. **Mom said that I should go to bed.** Indirect quotations often include words like **said that**. Do not use quotation marks around indirect quotations.

Label each quotation direct (D) or indirect (I). Put quotation marks around the direct quotations.

1. _____My favorite lunch is pizza, said Jeff.

2. _____Emily said that she prefers a burrito.

3. _____Jill asked me, What do you like?

4. _____I replied that my favorite is a hot meatball sandwich.

5. _____I asked my dad what he likes.

6. _____He answered, I love chicken noodle soup.

7. _____My mom said that she likes yogurt.

Use the Right Word!

Correct: *Juan and **I** swim well.* **Incorrect:** *Juan and **me** swim well.*
Correct: *Give Jen and **me** more.* **Incorrect:** *Give Jen and **I** more.*
To determine whether to use **I** or **me**, drop the other name in the sentence.
I swim well is correct, but **me swim well** is incorrect. **Give me more** is correct,
but **Give I more** is incorrect.

---

*Correct the following sentences. If **I** and **me** are used correctly, mark Ok.*

1. Bret and me like to play monopoly as a team.

2. My brother sold Bret and me Park Place.

3. Bret and me decided to buy Boardwalk.

4. Usually, my brother beats Bret and I.

5. This time, Bret and me thought we would win.

6. He and I waited for my brother to land on Boardwalk.

7. He never did, and Bret and me lost anyway.

Make It Right!

Correct six spelling mistakes, one capitalization mistake, and one incomplete sentence.

The night before christmas, I was just shuting my eyes when I heard

an funny taping noise. Jumped out of my bed and sneaked past

my brother who was snoring. At last I had a chance to meat Santa.

I found a old flashlight and switched it on. I didn't see Santa, but I

did see a snoplow throwing clumps of snow onto the window.

Spell It Right!

More Double Trouble

Underline the words that make the doubling rule correct.

When adding a suffix to a one-syllable word, double the final consonant of the root word when the suffix begins with a **(vowel, consonant)**, when the root word ends with one **(vowel, consonant)** followed by one **(vowel, consonant)**.

Add the suffix to the root word. Be sure to follow the doubling rule.

1. skip   -ed   _____

2. nap   -ing   _____

3. bad   -ly   _____

4. bleed   -ing   _____

5. snap   -ed   _____

6. sneak   -ing   _____

7. stop   -ing   _____

Write It Right!

Quotation Punctuation

Question marks and exclamation marks sometimes go inside quotation marks and sometimes go outside quotation marks. If the quotation itself is a question or an exclamation, then the punctuation goes inside the quotation marks. **"What's up, Doc?"** If the whole sentence is a **question** or **exclamation**, then the punctuation goes outside the quotation marks. **Who said "I have a dream?"** Periods and commas **always** go in front of quotation marks.

Add question marks and exclamation marks where necessary.

1. My friend whispered, " What are you doing after school "

2. "Be quiet " the teacher yelled.

3. Why do teachers yell, "Be quiet "

4. "What do you want to do " I asked.

5. She answered, "Do you want to go to the park "

6. The teacher said, "Are you talking about the park "

7. Who said, "I'm going to the park "

8. "Detention" shouted the teacher

Use the Right Word!

Word Order Review

Remember: **I** or **me** always comes after any other names. Ben and **I** are friends. Give it to Ben and **me**.

*Check and correct the use of **I** and **me** in the following sentences. If they are used correctly, mark OK.*

1. Me and Lisa like to talk on the telephone.

2. My mom yells at me and Lisa if we talk too long.

3. Lisa and I are in the same class.

4. Eliza and Molly play with Lisa and I.

5. Molly annoys me and Lisa sometimes.

6. Lisa and me are annoying too.

7. She and I stick together.

8. Sometimes Molly teases Eliza, Lisa, and me.

Make It Right!

Correct three spelling errors, four punctuation errors and two word order and usage errors.

Last weekend, my cousin and me went down to the beach to look

at the tide pools. Jim and me hopped, skiped, and jumped, threw

the surf to the rocks. Sneaking up to the edge of a pool, I peekked

in to find the crabs hiding there. A crab shouted If you stick your

hand in here, I'm going to snap it with my claws " I said to Jim, "Did

you hear that"?

What Have You Learned?

Check the spelling of the underlined words. Correct if necessary.

1. The <u>armys</u> <u>fought</u> in the <u>cities</u>.

2. The <u>tapping</u> noise <u>worryed</u> the <u>wolfs</u>.

3. The <u>sheeps</u> were <u>naping</u> under <u>a</u> oak tree.

4. <u>Father</u> <u>braught</u> the <u>frys</u> to the table.

5. I <u>remember</u> <u>stoping</u> to think about the <u>importent</u> question.

Add punctuation and capitalization where necessary.

6. I screamed get me out of here

7. She complained that she was tired

8. What did he mean when he said You are in trouble

Choose the incorrect segment. If there is no mistake, write OK.

9. I read / Where's Waldo? /when I was seven.
       a.   b.   c.

10. Rob and me / caught the /chicken pox together.
       a.   b.   c.

11. The teacher cought / Mark and me / talking again.
       a.   b.   c.

12. My favorite / book is <u>the / Black Stallion</u>.

       a.   b.   c.

Skill Check 21-25

What Have You Learned?

Check the spelling of the underlined words. Correct if necessary.

1. The <u>spys</u> were <u>worried</u> that they would be <u>caught</u>.

2. Twigs <u>snaped</u> as the <u>deers</u> <u>hopped</u> <u>through</u> the brush.

3. July 4 is <u>a</u> <u>impotant</u> <u>holliday</u> in the <u>United states</u>.

4. She <u>skiped</u> the section on <u>gooses</u>, <u>mooses</u>, and cabooses.

5. I <u>replyed</u> that I <u>thaught</u> she was terribly <u>snobbish</u>.

Add punctuation and capitalization where necessary.

6. My mother shouted time to get up

7. She said that it was late

8. She called do you want to be late

9. Why do mothers always say you are going to be late

Choose the incorrect segment. If there is no mistake write OK.

10. <u>The Wind In The</u> / <u>Willows</u> is a /really funny book.
            a.   b.   c.

11. My dad and me /often read /together at night.
            a.   b.   c.

12. My dad reads / <u>Treasure Island</u> to /me and my sister.
            a.   b.   c.

Get It Write **Right!**

What Have You Learned?

Descriptive words make interesting writing. "Come here," said Val, is a boring sentence. "Come here!" screamed Val, is much more interesting.

*Write five sentences with quotations. Instead of the word **said**, use some more descriptive words from the list below.*

whispered	shouted	screamed	nagged
muttered	gossiped	yelled	suggested
hissed	gasped	reported	sighed

_____

_____

_____

_____

_____

_____

_____

Spelling and Usage List 21-25

Spelling List 21–25

United States	spies	cities	batted	skipped
country	spied	donkeys	shipment	napping
America	carries	armies	shutting	badly
father	carried	parties	centered	bleeding
remember	hurries	days	tapping	snapped
important	hurried	monkeys	snobbish	sneaking
holiday	fries		hopped	stopping
	fried		peaking	
	worries		jumped	
	worried			
	replies			
	replied			

Usage List 21–25

went	bought	mice	I
saw	brought	moose	me
swam	thought	geese	
did	fought	wolves	
were	caught	sheep	
wrote	taught	lice	
		skunks	
		deer	

Review Question	Unit Practice	Skill Check Question	Unit Practice
1	23A, 22C	1	22A, 22C
2	24A, 22A, 23C	2	25A, 23C, 24A, 20C
3	23C, 25A, 18C	3	21A
4	21A, 22C, 22A	4	25A, 23C
5	21A, 25A	5	22A, 22C, 24A
6	22B, 23B, 25B	6	22B, 23B, 25B
7	24B	7	24B
8	22B, 23B, 25B	8	22B, 23B, 25B
9	21B	9	22B, 23B, 25B
10	24C, 25C	10	21B
11	22C, 24C, 25C	11	24C, 25C
12	21B	12	10C, 24C, 25C

Units 1-5

A Spelling   B Mechanics   C Usage   D Proofreading

1A High Frequency Words—page 1.
  1. b   2. c   3. a   4. b

1B Periods & Question Marks—page 2.
  1. .   2. ?   3. ?   4. .   5. ?

1C Subject-Verb Agreement—page 3.
  1. a   2. b   3. b   4. b

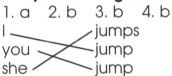

1D Proofreading—page 4.
  1. My dog look**s** at me.
     (or ...dogs look...)
  2. Do you want dinner**?**
  3. H**is** dish is full.
  4. He does not **like** his food.
  5. He want**s** ice cream.

2A Wh- Question Words—page 5.
  1. c   2. d   3. b   4. d   5. d

2B Capitalization—page 6.
  1. **M**y friend, **H**al, is taller than my sister.
  2. My sister, **J**an, is taller than **I** am.
  3. **M**y cat is shorter than my dog, **J**ack.
  4. **J**ack is also taller than **H**arry, my hermit crab.

  John, I, Mary, Ben

2C Subject-Verb Agreement—page 7.
  1. c   2. d   3. b   4. b

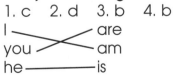

2D Proofreading—page 8.
  1. **W**ho sent me this gift**?**
  2. It **is** tied with a red ribbon.
  3. **What** do you think is in the box**?**
  4. **When** I open it, **I** will know.

3A Short Vowel Words—page 9.
  1. bed   2. fuzz   3. socks
  4. dust   5. helps

  Answers will vary.

  who, what, when, why, where

3B More Capitalization—page 10.
  1. Friday, February   2. February
  3. Wednesday   4. July
  5. The

  months, days

3C To, Too, Two—page 11.
  1. to   2. two   3. two   4. too
  5. two, too,   6. to, two.

3D Proofreading—page 12.
  1. I have **two** pets.
  2. I got my dog in **J**une and my snake last **T**uesday.
  3. **What** do you think my snake eats**?**
  4. She **eats** mice and rats **too**.
  5. Her name is **S**ally.
  6. **M**y dog's name **is** Harry.

4A Long Vowel Words—page 13.
  1. b   2. c   3. a   4. d   5. b

4B Using Commas—page 14.
  1. Monday, January 1, 1995.
  2. Hollywood, California.

A   Spelling   B   Mechanics   C   Usage   D   Proofreading

3. London, England.
4. Tuesday, February 28.
5. Rome, Italy,

4C Present & Past Tense—page 15.
1. smelled   2. walked   3. looked
4. leaned   5. jumped   6. wanted

4D Proofreading—page 16.
1. My birthday is **S**aturday,November 1.
2. I want **two** presents for my birthday.
3. I **hope** I will get a red **bike**.
4. Last year, I want**ed** a new gam**e**.
5. **What** do you want for your birthday**?**

5A Color Words—page 17.
green, yellow, black, purple, white,
orange, brown

5B Commas in a List—page 18.
1. dog, my cat, and fish.
2. Bongo, Jelly, and Finny.
3. Tara, Amber, and Pete
4. OK
5. cat, walk my dog, and feed my
   fish.

three

5C Blue, Blew, Red, Read—page 19.
1. blew   2. red (blue) 3. read
4. blue (red) 5. red...blue

5D Proofreading—page 20.
1. Her new dress is **green**, yellow,
   and blue.
2. Yesterday, the wind **blew** hard.
3. I **read two** books last month.
4. My pet **snake** has **yellow** stripes
   and spots.
5. The snow is **white** in Fairbanks,
   Alaska.

Review 1-5—page 21.
1. a   2. c   3. d
4. the movies**?**   5. **M**onday.
6. London**,** England.
7. Joe, Jim, and Jose
8. b   9. c   10. b

My dog rolled (rolls) in green slime.

Skill Check 1-5—page 22.
1. b   2. c   3. a
4. My friend **Jill**   5. come **too**?
6. **T**hursday   7. Portland, Maine
8. b   9. a   10. c

Do you like to **bake** cookies**?**

You Write It 1-5—page 23.
Answers will vary

6A Consonant Blend Words—page 25.
1. b   2. b   3. b   4. a   5. b

**6B More Periods & Question Marks
—page 26.**
1. .   2. ?   3. .   4. .   5. ?

**6C More Subject-Verb Agreement
—page 27.**
1. b   2. a   3. b   4. b

verb

6D. Proofreading—page 28.
1. Do you know how to swim**?**
2. I am scared to **swim**.
3. My father swim**s** very fast.
4. Does a shark swim faster**?**
5. A sunburn makes my skin **red**.

7A High Frequency Words—page 29.
1. b   2. c   3. c   4. d   5. d

7B Titles—page 30.
1. My teacher, **Mr. C**hen, is very tall.

2. My doctor, **Dr. W**hite, is quite fat.
3. Mrs. **C**ruz has long ears.
4. M**s**. Smoot is very pretty.

Mr.   James   **Dr.**   I   M**s.**   **M**rs.

7C More Subject-Verb Agreement —page 31.

1. b   2. b   3. b   4. b   5. b

7D Proofreading—page 32.

1. My dentist, Dr. **T**ooth, is a silly woman.
2. She make**s** a face when she look**s** at my teeth.
3. A big smile of clean w**h**ite te**e**th is pretty.
4. B**r**ush your teeth **two** times a day to keep them clean.

8A More Consonant Blend Words —page 33.

1. break   2. cross   3. walk
4. step   5. stuff

8B Comma Practice—page 34.

1. drink, a sandwich,
2. January 1,
3. Trenton,
4. Thursday,
5. peas, beans,

8C Irregular Verbs—page 35.

1. went   2. saw   3. had
4. broke   5. were   6. took
7. got

8D Proofreading—page 36.

1. Yesterday, I **went to** the zoo.
2. I saw the lions, elephants, and bears.

3. The elephants **were** spraying water with their **trunks**.
4. One elephant sprayed **Mr.** Lopez.
5. His clothes **were** soaked.
6. Do you **think** the elephants were laughing**?**

9A High Frequency Words—page 37.

1. b   2. c   3. d   4. d   5. b

9B Punctuation Practice—page 38.

Ms. Jenkins was born in Paris, France on January 1, 1974. She is a great teacher. We have French cakes, cookies, and bread in class sometimes. Have you ever had them? They are yummy.

9C Word Order—page 39.

1. Boobies are **very odd** birds.
2. Some boobies **have** bright blue feet.
3. When a boy booby wants to **show off**, he lifts his feet.
4. Girl boobies like the boys **with the** bright blue feet.
5. Blue-footed boobies **are very** proud of their silly feet.
6. Their feet don't **look silly** to other boobies.

9D Proofreading—page 40.

1. Mrs. Kim is my soccer coach.
2. **This** year, we **could** be champs.
3. We are working on dribbling**,** shooting, and heading the ball.
4. We meet at my **school** and play games at the high **school**.
5. We **will** win our next **game**.

10A Color Crosswords—page 41.

Across		Down	
2	red	1	yellow
5	purple	3	brown
6	white	4	blue

10B Capitalization and Punctuation —page 42.

Dr. **D**oomsday was born in **F**ritz, **G**ermany on **O**ctober 13, 1945. **H**e is very ugly, cruel, and sneaky. **H**e plans to blow up the world. **W**e have our own secret weapon. **H**e is a superhero.

10C Word Order—page 43.

1. Jen and I
2. my brother and me
3. Sarah and I
4. Joe, Jack, and I
5. Ryan, Emma, and me

after

10D Proofreading—page 44.

1. Should **Jill and I** go with Brad**?**
2. They painted my **school yellow**.
3. Juan **was grumpy** and sad yesterday.
4. Dr. Jones wears a **white** coat.
5. The falling bricks **could** hurt **Jake and me**.

Review 6-10—page 45.

1. c　2. b　3. c　4. too?
5. December 31, 1940.
6. Dr. Dog　7. Will, Ben, and I
8. b　9. a　10. c

Mrs. **S**mith, the nurse, gave **my brother and me** a shot.

Skill Check 6-10—page 46.

1. a　2. b　3. c　4. Mr. Perkins,
5. OK　6. Thursday, February 1.
7. Jon, Bess, and me.
8. c　9. b　10. b

In Flagstaff, Arizona, it is **too** cold to go outside today.

You Write It 6-10—page 47.

Answers will vary

11A Numbers—page 49.

1. seven　2. two　3. four　4. three
5. nine　6. one　7. eight　8. zero

11B Dear Uncle Sam—page 50.

Dear Bad Guys,
Sincerely yours,
Spider Man

Dear Mr. Hanson,
Can you repair my cape**?**
I think I need a bigger size.
Regards,
Superman

11C Which is Witch?—page 51.

1. won, **one**　2. too, **two**
3. for, **four**　4. no, **know**
5. eight, **ate**

11D Proofreading—page 52.

6 Forest Lane
Woody Lake, Michigan
July 9, 2005

Dear Grandma,
May I visit you next week**?** I want to walk over to your house on Saturday. My mom says that the woods are scary. Have you seen any bears, lions, or tigers**?**
Love,
Little Red RH

12A High Frequency Words—page 53.

1. d　2. c　3. c　4. a　5. b

12B Complete Sentences—page 54.

(Answers may vary.)

Jean and the elephant　was hot.
The elephant　like to play..
The other kids　runs really fast.
Usually, the winner　was hard to..
The afternoon　could find..

A Spelling   B Mechanics   C Usage   D Proofreading

12C Bee or Be?—page 55.
1. bee, be   2. hour, our   3. buy, by
4. whole, hole   5. sent, cent

12D Proofreading—page 56.
July 6, 2005
Dear Mom and Dad,
Camp is really fun. We run **around**
all night. At the campfire, I ate
about **four** hundred marshmallows.
I had a bellyache. We have lots of
different things **to** do here.
Love,
Taylor

13A Contractions—page 57.
1. d   2. b   3. a   4. b   5. b

13B Exclamations!—page 58.
1. ?   2. .   3. !   4. ? 5. ?
6. !   7. !   8. .   9. .

13C Verb Tenses—page 59.
kick   kicked   will kick
work   worked   will work
climb   climbed   will climb
thump   thumped   will thump
spook   spooked   will spook

13D Proofreading—page 60.
Yikes**!** The ground is shaking. Have
you ever felt an earthquake**?** If
you feel an earthquake, you
shouldn't run outside. You should
stand in a doorway or sit under a
table so things **won't** fall on you. It
will be over in **two** minutes.

14A Verb Endings—page 61.
1. painted   2. hoped   3. cracked
4. jumped   5. raced   6. looked
7. snooped   8. freed   9. snarled
10. replaced

**14B More complete Sentences
—page 62.**
(Answers will vary.)
1. Subject ...mole dug a tunnel.
2. Predicate He digs...
3. Predicate The mole pokes...
4. Subject ...home is safe.
5. b
6. a

14C Irregular Verbs—page 63.
eat, **ate; have**, had; know, **knew;**
sit, **sat;** drink, **drank; come**, came;
speak, spoke

14D Proofreading—page 64.
3 Forest Lane
Woodland, PA
May 3, 2005

Dear Mr. and Mrs. Bear,
I'm sorry I **went** into your house and
ate your porridge. I didn't know
that the chair would break when I
sat in it. I cried all last night. **I** want
to say how sorry I am.
Regretfully,
Goldilocks

15A High Frequency Words—page 65.
1. high   2. high enough
3. While   4. thought
5. Should, should 6. should, whole

15B Capitalize Holidays—page 66.
1. Halloween   2. Mother's Day
3. Day, Sunday, May
4. Fourth of July   5. fall
6. winter, Christmas, Friday, December

15C More Irregular Words—page 67.
1. gave   2. fall   3. sang
4. was   5. brings 6. said, was

15D Proofreading—page 68.

August 16, 2005
Dear Aunt Jenny,
Thank you very much for the new game you sent on **M**emorial **D**ay. It is so cool**!** It **should** keep me busy all summer. **I** **thought** I **knew** how to play it, but I was wrong. **It** is difficult.
I hope you are having a fun **s**ummer.
Love,
Marcie

Review 11-15—page 69.

1. two   2. bees   3. enough
4. sat   5. spoke, sang

Answers will vary
6. Incomplete   7. Incomplete   8. OK

June 6, 2005
Dear **S**ir,
I **sent** away for the action figure advertised on your cereal box. You **said** it was life sized, but it was**n't** even three inches **high**. I am so angry**!** I want my money back.
Sincerely,
Thomas

Skill Check 11-15—page 70.

1. different, children   2. knew
3. While, whole   4. couldn't

Answers will vary
5. Incomplete   6. OK
7. Incomplete

October 12, 2005
Dear Mr. Mendez,
I am making a haunted house in my garage for **H**alloween. I will need to rent **two** mummies and **three** skeletons. It will be scary**!** Last **s**pring, you **said** you would help me. Is the offer still good**?**
Sincerely,
Madison

You Write It 11-15—page 71.

Answers will vary

16A Compound words—page 73.

1. rowboat   2. bedtime
3. hotdog   4. snowplow
5. highway   6. downtown

16B ABCDEFGHIJKLMNO...—page 74.

1. Bob   2. Cathy   3. Juan
4. Teddy

1. Mrs. Aardvark   2. Mr. Zebra
3. Ms. Kangaroo   4. Miss Wombat

16C Homonyms—page 75.

1. no   2. sea   3. bear
4. meat   5. tail   6. hear

16D Proofreading—page 76.

If you are lucky, you can see something odd down at the beach in **J**anuary. Sometimes a huge whale will jump out of the **sea**. His **tail** looks as big as a skyscraper. **He m**akes a splash like a tidal **wave**. Sometimes you can even **hear** the noises the whales make. Do you **know** what they are saying**?**

17A More Compound Words—page 77.

sunset, sailboat, rainbow, paycheck, mailman, backpack, watchband, earring

rope, Miami, doctor

17B ABCDEFGHIJKLMNO...—page 78.

Bart,   Ben,   Bill,   Bob,   Bret

Bab**ara**   Bab**s**

17C More Irregular Verbs—page 79.

1. grew   2. began   3. was
4. found   5. told   6. said
7. verb   8. noun

17D Proofreading—page 80.
1. a   2. b   3. b   4. c   5. c   6. a
7. b   8. b

18A More Verb Endings—page 81.
he sniffs, she catches, it smashes, she walks, he kisses, he passes, she laughs

18B More Complete Sentences —page 82.
1. I / watch   2. My eyes / get
3. The ads / seem
4. Too many people / believe
5. C   6. I   7. I   8. C

and <u>man</u> <u>room</u> hot <u>giraffe</u>

18C A or An?—page 83.
How to Make **an** Awful Mess
a bucket, **a** quart, **a** bottle, **an** enormous, **an** entire, **a** helping, **an** hour

18D Proofreading—page 84.
One kid at my school is **an** awful bully. Every time he **passes** me in the hall, he **laughs** at me. **He** bosses everyone around. Sometimes at lunch, he walks by the tables and **smashes** my sandwiches. My friend Jim never walks past him if he can avoid it. Some day, when a teacher **catches** him, he is going to be in trouble. He thinks he is cool, but he is **an** ugly troll.

19A High Frequency Words—page 85.
1. b   2. d   3. c   4. d   5. d
6. b   7. d

19B Punctuation Review—page 86.
34 Green Grover Lane
Emerald City, OZ 92034
June 2, 2005

Dear Dr. Dimwit,
I am having trouble with my new brain. It doesn't seem to work very well. I had an x-ray taken, and it looked a lot like a cabbage. Is it supposed to look that way**?** When I have the straw replaced next time, please check my heart, my liver, and my kidneys too.
Sincerely yours,
Moe Scarecrow

person, place, thing

19C Verb Tenses—page 87.

Present T.	Future T.	Past T.
run	will run	**ran**
write	will write	**wrote**
am	will be	was
freeze	will freeze	**froze**
say	will say	**said**
hide	**will hide**	hid
do	will do	**did**

19D Proofreading—page 88.
Last night I had **an** awful dream. I was with a **group** of kids in my classroom. I wanted to go out to recess **really** badly, but the teacher wouldn't let me go. He **said** I had to **answer several** questions first. I **found** the answers in my science book, **wrote** them down, and **ran** outside, but recess was already over. What a terrible dream!

20A Plural Nouns—page 89.
cakes, dishes, glasses, cows, foxes, matches, snakes, sandwiches

20B More ABCDEFGHIJKLM...—page 90.
1. b   2. e   3. a   4. d   5. c   6. c
7. e   8. b

A   Spelling   B   Mechanics   C   Usage   D   Proofreading

___

20C More Homonyms—page 91.
1. made   2. wood   3. too
4. through   5. there   6. would
7. threw   8. too   9. to
10. their

20D Proofreading—page 92.
My friend's mother, **Mrs.** James, has a thing about cows. She has cows on her **dishes** and glasses. She fills **their** house with cows **made** of wood and plastic. I don't think cows are so **great**. I prefer **foxes** and snakes myself. Imagine **beautiful** glasses and **dishes** decorated with big, long snakes with poisonous fangs!

Review 16-20—page 93
1. Do you **really** **know** the <u>answer</u>?
2. She **catches** the ball and <u>throws</u> it **through** the grass.
3. A <u>rainbow</u> floated over the **highway**.
4. **An** ice storm **froze** my nose and toes.
5. Ben   6. Pat   7. Paul

Who **would** believe it? My friend **told** me a **tale** so silly that I laughed. He **said** that he **found** some pirate gold in a cave by the **sea**. Pirates hid **their** gold in a small **wood** chest there. I think my friend is watching **too** many movies.

Skill Check 16—20–page 94.
1. Her **earring** and <u>watchband</u> are **made** of gold.
2. The **foxes** hid in **their** burrow.
3. My shirt **matches** my <u>skirt</u> and socks **too**.
4. Make up <u>a</u> <u>tale</u> about **an** ant and <u>a</u> butterfly.
5. Elmer   6. Jared   7. John
8. Ricky

Last winter was **a** cold one. The lake **froze**, and the **highways** were covered with ice. **Would** spring ever come? Finally, in **March**, I saw a green leaf sticking **through** the snow. On the first warm day, my friends **threw** off **their** coats and hats. Spring was **here** at last!

You Write It 16-20—page 95.
Answers will vary

21A High Frequency Words—page 97.
1. c   2. b   3. b   4. b   5. c
6. c   7. b

21B Book Titles—page 98.
1. <u>Tales of a Fourth Grade Nothing.</u>
2. <u>The Hobbit.</u>
3. <u>Into Thin Air.</u>
4. <u>Art Through the Ages.</u>
5. <u>Freckle Juice.</u>

21C More Irregular Verbs—page 99.
1. b   2. c   3. a   4. b   5. c
6. c

add <u>d</u>.

21D Proofreading—page 100.
When I was little, I loved books by Dr. Seuss. I **sat** for hours listening to <u>Green Eggs and Ham</u>. I **remember** my dad **sang** it to me just before I **went** to bed. He **knew** it by heart. Did you have a favorite bedtime story?

22A Verbs Ending in -Y—page 101

Present Tense	Present Tense	Past Tense
I spy	He spies	I spied
You carry	He **carries**	I **carried**
We hurry	Bill **hurries**	He **hurried**
I fry	He **fries**	We **fried**
You worry	She **worries**	They **worried**
They rely	He **replies**	Marge **replied**

22B Quotation Marks—page 102.

1. My mom called out, "Time to go."
2. She said, "Get your backpack."
3. She added, " You have soccer practice after school."
4. She nagged, "Pick up those socks."
5. She says the same thing every morning: "Don't forget your lunch."

22C More Irregular Verbs—page 103.

1. bought   2. brought   3. thought
4. fought   5. caught   6. taught

a <u>verb</u>.

22D Proofreading—page 104.

I **got** in big trouble with my sister yesterday. She **brought** home a library book, <u>The Land of Dinosaurs</u>, that looked really interesting. I was looking at it in the **bathroom** when she knocked on the door. She yelled, **"**Hurry up, Jimmy**!"** Then she started pounding on the door. **"**I need to get in there**!"**

"Wait a minute,**"** I **replied**. By mistake, I dumped the book into the tub. Oh, oh!

<u>jump</u>

23A Nouns Ending in -Y—page 105.

Singular	Consonant then -Y?	Vowel then -Y	Plural
donkey	no	yes	donkeys
army	yes	no	armies
party	yes	no	parties
day	no	yes	days
monkey	no	yes	monkeys

23B More Quotations—page 106.

1. Jenna said, "**M**y dog…
2. Bill added, "**M**y homework …
3. …on the way to school," claimed…
4. …with my homework," complained…
5. Chad said, "**A**liens…
6. …a bit silly," replied…
7. She added, "I…

23C Moose, Mice, Meese?—page 107.

1. mice   2. moose   3. geese
4. wolves   5. sheep   6. lice
7. skunks   8. deer

a noun

23D Proofreading—page 108.

1. b   2. a   3. b   4. b   5. a   6. c
7. c   8. a

24A Double Trouble—page 109

batted   shipment   shutting

Root	Suf. Vow.	One Syll.	1 Short Vow.	1 Final Con.	Dbl.?
bat	yes	yes	yes	yes	yes
ship	no	yes	yes	yes	no
shut	yes	yes	yes	yes	yes
center	yes	no	yes	yes	no
tap	yes	yes	yes	yes	yes
snob	yes	yes	yes	yes	yes
hop	yes	yes	yes	yes	yes
peak	yes	yes	no	yes	no
jump	yes	yes	yes	no	no

A Spelling   B Mechanics   C Usage   D Proofreading

batted   shipment   shutting
centered   tapping   snobbish
hopped   peaking   jumped

24B Indirect Quotations—page 110.
1. D "My favorite...pizza," said Jeff.
2. I   3. D Jill asked me, "What...like?"
4. I   5. I
6. D He answered, "I...soup."   7. I

24C I or Me—page 111.
1. Bret and I   2. OK   3. Bret and I
4. Bret and me   5. Bret and I
6. OK   7. Bret and I

24D Proofreading—page 112.
The night before **C**hristmas, I was just **shutting** my eyes when I heard **a** funny **tapping** noise. **I** jumped out of my bed and sneaked past my brother who was snoring. At last I had a chance to **meet** Santa. I found **an** old flashlight and switched it on. I didn't see Santa, but I did see a **snowplow** throwing clumps of snow onto the window.

25A More Double Trouble—page 113.
vowel, vowel, consonant
1. skipped   2. napping 3. badly
4. bleeding 5. snapped
6. sneaking 7. stopping

25B Quotation Punctuation—page 114.
1. ...after school?"
2. "Be quiet!" the ...
3. ..."Be quiet"?
4. ...want to do?" I asked
5. ...go to the park?"
6. ...about the park?"
7. ...to the park"?
8. "Detention!" shouted...

25C Word Order Review—page 115.
1. Lisa and I   2. Lisa and me
3. OK   4. Lisa and me

5. Lisa and me   6. Lisa and I
7. OK   8. OK

25D Proofreading—page 116.
Last weekend, my cousin and **I** went down to the beach to look at the tide pools. Jim and **I** hopped, **skipped**, and jumped **through** the surf to the rocks. Sneaking up to the edge of a pool, I **peeked** in to find the crabs hiding there. A crab shouted**,** "If you stick your hand in here, I'm going to snap it with my claws**!**" I said to Jim, "Did you hear that**?**"

Review 21-25—page 117.
1. armies
2. worried, wolves
3. sheep, napping, an
4. brought, fries
5. stopping, important
6. I screamed, "Get me out of here!"
7. She complained that she was tired.
8. What did he mean when he said, "You are in trouble"?
9. b   10. a   11. a   12. b

Skill Check 21-25—page 118.
1. spies,
2. snapped, deer
3. an, important,holiday, United States
4. skipped, geese, moose
5. replied, thought
6. My mother shouted, "**T**ime to get up!"
7. She said that it was late.
8. She called, "**D**o you want to be late?"
9. Why do mothers always say, "**Y**ou are going to be late"?
10. a   11. a   12. c

You Write It 21-25—page 119
Answers will vary.